EDWARD MACDOWELL

Piano Concerto No. 2
in D minor

Ed. 3478 (Formerly Library Vol. 1462)

G. SCHIRMER, Inc.

DISTRIBUTED BY

 HAL•LEONARD®
CORPORATION

7777 W. BLUEMOUND RD. P.O. BOX 13819 MILWAUKEE, WI 53213

To Mme. Teresa Carreño

Piano Concerto No. 2
in D minor

I

Edited by Edwin Hughes

Edward MacDowell. Op. 23

Copyright © 1922 G. Schirmer, Inc.
Copyright renewed by G. Schirmer, Inc.
All Rights Reserved   International Copyright Secured   Printed in U.S.A.
This work may not be reproduced or transmitted in whole or in part in any form
or by any means, electronic or mechanical, including photocopying or by any
information storage and retrieval system, without permission in writing from
the publisher.

48617c

Poco piu mosso, e con passione

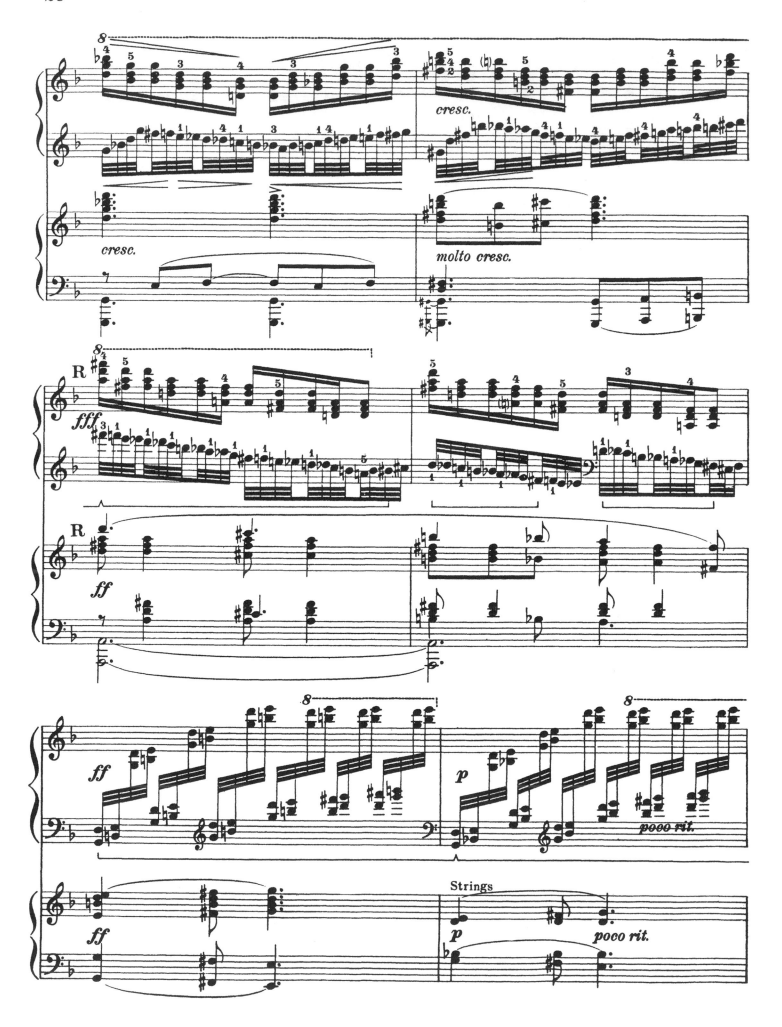

II

III

Str.